NOTHING
BUT LOVE

NOTHING

BUT LOVE

Health and Holiness through
Intimacy with God

ROBERT E. LAUDER

Resurrection Press
Mineola • New York

To Pat and Henry
with loving gratitude
for many years of friendship

Grateful acknowledgment is made to *The Long Island Catholic*
for material that first appeared in its pages.

First published in 1993 by Resurrection Press, Ltd.
P.O. Box 248
Williston Park, NY 11596

ISBN 1-878718-16-9

Cover design by John Murello

Printed in the United States of America.

Contents

~ 1 ~

God:
Community of Love

I can't remember the first time I heard the expression "identity crisis" but I know that I have heard it with increasing frequency in the last few years. I hear people make statements like "I have to find myself" or "I'm trying to get my act together" or even "I am experiencing some kind of conversion."

In any kind of identity crisis some certainties fail. Some things which were once very clear seem to be blurred. What once was steady ground is now a little like quicksand. At times the identity crisis happens suddenly and dramatically but it can also creep up on us. Over a relatively long period of time an erosion of certainties occurs and we realize that we are undergoing some kind of change, some kind of growth experience — at least we hope it is a growth experience. An identity crisis can be an opportunity for growth but it does not have to be. Unfortunately the crisis might lead to regression. We may move backward rather than forward.

The type of identity crisis that interests me most is the type that is related to a person's spirituality. Our identity comes about through our relationships. We are made who we are through our relatives, our teachers, our friends. The more important the relationship the more influential it is in bringing about our identity. This is why the parent-child relationship is so important. I guess it is impossible to overemphasize the influence that our parents have on us. We carry our parents inside us throughout our lives. Other important relationships can have an enormous effect on us. Some marriage partners profoundly affect the personalities of their spouses. Frequently we hear remarks such as, "He is so different since he married her." The intimacy of the marriage relationship can cause dramatic changes in the personalities of some people.

As Christians we are supposed to take our religious identity from the risen Lord. Catholics believe that Jesus is God's message to the human race. What God wants us to know he has revealed through his Son. From Jesus we can learn something about God and we can learn about ourselves. If we remind ourselves that everything that Jesus does he does as Son of God then we can realize that everything that Jesus does tells us something about the Father. When Jesus heals the man born blind that tells us something about the Father; when Jesus forgives the woman caught in adultery that tells us something about the Father; when Jesus performs the miracle at the marriage feast of Cana that tells us something about the Father; when Jesus raised Lazarus from the dead that tells us something about the Father. Jesus' identity is Son of God and so he is always acting as Son of the Father. Because God's Son has become incarnate Jesus' actions are also telling us about how we should live. The God-man reveals both God and man to us.

In relation to a religious identity crisis I think that one of the most illuminating scenes in the gospel is the scene in the Garden of Gethsemane. Jesus does not want to die. Everything in him rebels at the thought of death. He is frightened. If at all possible he wants to stay alive. Jesus prays and delivers himself up to his Father and trusts him. Jesus does die but his Father raises him from the dead and Jesus enters into risen life. The scene in the Garden can tell us much about what our religious identity should be.

We are called to surrender to Jesus' Father and our Father. Our basic relationship to God should be one of trust. The Father who led Jesus through death to a new way of living will sustain us and nourish us no matter what crises we experience.

Since Vatican Council II, Catholics have experienced many changes in their lives. My guess is that the changes are going to continue. Whether we like or dislike the changes we should not forget what is basic to our faith — like Jesus we place our trust in our heavenly Father. We are loved by our Father more than we can imagine. We are the beloved of God. That more than anything else gives us our identity.

This small book is an attempt at reflecting on the mystery of personal existence in the light of Christian revelation.

Let's start with something that is very mysterious: God's involvement with us. Like God himself or herself, God's involvement with us is mysterious. My observation of myself and of other believers is that we tend to go to one of two extremes when we think of God being involved in our lives; we either think of God as so involved that he is really running our lives, or we think of God as so distant that he plays no role in our lives at all.

Some of us attribute everything that happens in our lives to God. We think that God directly sends everything that turns out well in our lives and that he also sends everything that turns out ill. For example, I can recall hearing believers say that jobs that they obtained or awards that they received were due to God. I have also heard believers comment on many unfortunate events that occur in their lives as crosses being sent by God. I suppose that second example bothers me more than the first, but attributing both good happenings and bad happenings directly to God presents problems for me.

My problem is that this view of God seems to overlook the reality of freedom, our own freedom and the freedom of others. For example, perhaps I was promoted or received a raise or award because I worked very hard for it or because my employer liked me. Instead of thinking of God as directly intervening at every moment, it makes more sense to me to recall that people are free and that free decisions do account for some of the good things that happen in our lives. I am quite ready to stress that freedom is a gift from God; and because God has given us that gift, we and other human beings are the cause of some of the good things that happen in our lives.

Thinking that God directly sends bad things into our lives presents even more problems. It is difficult to reconcile a God of love with a God who deliberately does bad things to the creatures he loves. For example, why would God send a tragedy into the life of someone he loves?

Once we stop saying that God directly intervenes in our lives in such a way that he is really running our lives, some of us go the opposite extreme and think that he is not involved at all. I think that the truth, which I admit is quite mysterious and beyond our ability to comprehend completely, is that God is involved in our lives in a way that is much better than the direct involvement that would take away our freedom.

God's presence in our lives is not a physical presence that forces us to act in a particular manner but rather a *loving* presence that calls and supports us to grow in freedom and to become more loving people. In human relationships love always frees the beloved, and this can give us a clue concerning how God is present to us. God's loving presence will free us and sanctify us if we open ourselves to him, love him and co-operate with his love. God's presence in our lives is a gently loving presence that will never force or coerce us to do anything. It is a presence that will enormously help us to act freely and lovingly.

God has decided to create us at least partly material which means that we might suffer either because of blind material forces like viruses or hurricanes or because of other free human beings who either choose to hurt us or inadvertently hurt us.

However we think of suffering, it is not necessary nor, I think, proper to think of God as directly sending it to us. However, it is more than proper to believe that when suffering comes, God's loving presence can see us through it.

God is more involved in our lives than we can ever understand. He is certainly involved in a way better than if he were moving us about as though we were robots. God's involvement is one of redeeming love.

It seems strange that the Blessed Trinity should in one way be at the center of the consciousness of Catholics but in another way be at the periphery of our consciousness. Every Catholic begins almost every prayer by blessing himself or herself — indicating that the Trinity is at the center of our belief. Indeed making the sign of the cross is an action which distinguishes Catholics from most other Christian believers.

Yet it seems that many Catholics shuffle the Trinity away from the center of their spiritual lives, feeling perhaps that whether or not God is one person or three persons makes little practical difference in the life of a struggling believer. This is unfortunate. That God is three persons and that God revealed his inner life to us should have important implications for our living of the Christian life.

I think that there are several approaches that we might take in trying to grasp more deeply the significance of the Trinity and enter more deeply into the inner life of God.

One way would be to reflect on the emphasis in the world and the Church today on relationships. We frequently hear people talking about how they are "working" on their relationships. We seem to sense in a new way that what is central to human living is relating to others — to other human persons and to God.

Our greatest material possessions cannot compare with the beauty of the important relationships in our lives. What God has revealed to us is that he is also involved in relating. God's inner life is a community of love. The greatest philosophers and thinkers were not able to discover this truth about God. We only know about it because God has decided to share his community life with us, to tell us about himself and to invite us to enter into the intimate loving community he is.

The most fruitful way for the Christian to approach the inner life of God is through Jesus. Everything Jesus did in his earthly life he did as Son. Jesus is the Word of God, the message of God to us. Jesus does not just tell us the Good News; he is the Good News. He does not just tell us who God is by his speech; he tells us who God is by everything that he does. Jesus heals as Son, he preaches as Son, he prays as Son, he dies as Son. Jesus as Son is constantly revealing to us what his Father is like. The kindness and compassion of Jesus for the suffering and the needy tell us about his Father.

When Jesus leaves the apostles he sends his Spirit, the Spirit of Love. We come to know the Spirit first by looking at what the Spirit has accomplished in Jesus and then by considering what the Spirit accomplishes in the Church. The Holy Spirit works through our humanity to build the Kingdom of God. It is through the power of the Spirit that the Christian is able to live a life of faith and to reach out in charity to help others.

Some people spend their lives searching for God. As a priest I have frequently talked to people who seem to want to believe but for some reason are unable to believe. Talking to such people can be heartbreaking. What it is that prevents them from believing, that blocks their act of faith, is unknown to me. But when I do talk to such people I am usually moved to feel grateful for the faith which I have received as a gift. I suggest that this might be our basic reaction to the God who tells us who he really is. Our God is not a distant God for whom we must search: our God has taken us into the divine love community and allowed us to relate in love to the three divine persons in that community.

The Church is a community of free persons. What happens in the Church is a combination of God's grace and our free choices. God deals with us through a community. Part of the mystery of God for Christians is that God relates to Jesus' followers through a community.

I have an ongoing argument with some of my friends concerning the value of people leading a contemplative life. Some of my friends cannot understand what good is done just by praying. My friends think that those in contemplative religious orders should be active in tackling some of the problems that plague us. I argue that no one knows the good that is accomplished through prayer. From the time of early Christianity some followers of Jesus have felt called to leave the world and to live a life of prayer. I think that within the Christian community there will always be such people. At least I hope so.

A contemplative nun wrote me a letter a few years ago about an article I had written in the diocesan newspaper. The article was about the four women murdered in El Salvador in 1980. One of the four women murdered was Sister Ita Ford, a Maryknoll Sister. The contemplative Sister had prepared Ita for her First Communion. The more I think about that the more I marvel at the communal nature of the Church. The contemplative, who has spent her entire adult life behind convent walls engaged in prayer, prepared a little girl for her First Communion. Years later that little girl now grown up goes to El Salvador and dies as a Christian witness to the needs of the poor.

Who knows what seeds the contemplative sister planted in the heart of that seven-year old, seeds that came to fruition years later in martyrdom? Who knows what inspiration that contemplative Sister received and was able to use in instructing her young student? And who knows how many countless people will be inspired by the contemporary martyr and encouraged to give themselves to lives of service? We are a community and it is through this community that God deals with us.

We will never understand God completely nor will we ever understand completely his activity within his Church. We do know that God has decided to allow us to influence one another. God could have decided to deal with us as individuals but he has decided to deal with us through community. This means that each of us has responsibilities to the community. We are Christ's Body. We can think of that as a burden but it really is a magnificent privilege that we can be renewed and inspired through the community.

For various reasons each of us who is trying to live the Christian life focuses on different aspects of the mystery of God. In recent years the vulnerability of God has become more real to me. Who could have ever guessed that God would make himself vulnerable because of his love for us? Some of the greatest philosophers of all time never even came close to that truth. In Jesus we see God making himself vulnerable. From the moment of his Incarnation, God depends on his creatures. He made himself vulnerable even unto death.

During the last few years I have been made acutely aware of our vulnerability through the deaths of several people I knew. The news of a death is always a shock — whether the death comes suddenly and unexpectedly or whether it is expected. There seems to be such a finality to death. Often seconds after I hear of a death I think "I will never see that person again on this earth" and the thought calls to my mind just how fragile and finite we are.

Not long ago I had to go for two special medical tests. In each case there was little danger that the symptoms that led to the test were anything serious but in both cases the doctors wanted to be sure. In both cases I was relatively confident that

I did not have anything seriously wrong with me but still the experience of taking the tests vividly reminded me how vulnerable I am. People whom you do not know personally are examining you and undergoing the test caused me anxiety. I was very aware that I am not completely in control of my whole life and I realized once again that no matter how well we take care of ourselves there will come a moment for each and every one of us when we will have to hand ourselves over to our Father. Our vulnerability reminds us that we are called to trust in our Father and that the moment will come when that trust will be our final act. At some moment in each of our lives our health will depart and death will seem to win. The victory will only be apparent. Our trust in our Father will not have been in vain.

The vulnerability of Jesus reveals that God cares about us so much that he is ready to subject himself to his creatures; the resurrection of Jesus reveals that trusting in God will eventually lead to conquest — even of death.

The more I think about the mystery of the resurrection the more I have come to see it as the most meaningful revelation of who God is and who we are. In reflecting on Jesus' death and resurrection we have an opportunity to probe deeply into the mystery of the God who loves us. You do not have to live a very long time or have a vast number of human experiences to become aware that the existence of evil poses terribly difficult problems if we try to make sense of the world and our place in it. Almost every human being at some difficult point in his or her life asks, "Why do the good suffer? Why is there evil?" I do not know of any better way of reflecting on the presence of evil in human life than to reflect on it in the light of the death and resurrection of Jesus.

As we try to know God better and to understand him more, we have to face the truth that God allows some terrible things to happen to those he loves. There was no one whom God loved more than Jesus, his Incarnate Son, but God allowed his Son to be tortured and killed. Not only did God allow this to happen, but this suffering and death became the means through which the rest of the human race was redeemed from sin. We have heard this from our earliest years, and unfortunately we can neglect to allow it to illuminate our experience of life, of suffering and of death.

I think that we have to take the Incarnation seriously and remind ourselves that Jesus was not play acting when he was in the Garden of Gethsemane or when he was scourged or when he was on the cross. Jesus really suffered and really died. Reflection on the suffering and death of Jesus should convince us that neither our love for God nor God's love for us indicated that in this world we will never suffer. Not only does God allow those whom he loves to experience pain and disappointment but followers of Jesus are baptized into Jesus's death. How this will work out in the life of a Christian believer will vary enormously depending on all sorts of accidental factors, but the believer must be ready to pay whatever price is demanded for following Jesus.

Of course to focus only on Jesus' death and on the suffering of his followers would be to miss the great sign of God's love for us: the resurrection. In the risen Lord we see not only the victory over sin and the triumph of Jesus but also the goal that God intends for all of us. The resurrection of Jesus reveals how much God loves us.

We can make many true statements about God but no clear statements because God is radical mystery. We say that God is Love and we know that he is infinite love. What is infinite love? I know that every person whom I have met loves in a limited and finite way. What does it mean, not only to love in an infinite way, but to be Infinite Love? I really do not understand infinite love, but I believe that the resurrection of Jesus is a great sign of what it means.

In the risen Lord we have a sign that no matter how much suffering we endure or how much tragedy we experience, God's love will be sufficient for us. The resurrection of Jesus means that suffering and pain and disappointment and death are not the final word about human living. The final word about human living is that God is passionately in love with each of us and has arranged for his love relationship with us to last for eternity.

~ 2 ~

Persons: Poor but Never Alone

As I think back to my first few years as a priest I am amazed at how naive I was. As a student in the seminary I was interested in psychology and read a few books about it but I really knew very little. It is difficult for me to remember what I thought the relationship was between psychology and the spiritual life. I know that I believed then as I do now that grace builds on nature and that a psychologically and emotionally healthy person has a better chance to allow the fruits of grace to blossom in his or her life than a person who has crippling psychological or emotional problems. I do not recall whether my thoughts about psychology went much further than that. My experience as a parish priest quickly taught me that often what I tended to identify as a moral or spiritual problem had a psychological component to it.

In his very interesting and provocative study, *The Culture of Narcissism*, Christopher Lasch talks about what he calls the therapeutic personality. By it he means the self-centered personality that believes the world revolves around it and that all its needs should be immediately fulfilled. He charts its appearance through a misunderstanding of psychological therapy that has been influential in this country for the last few decades. There is a way of understanding therapy that reduces it to a narcissistic exercise that makes the patient more self-centered rather than less self-centered. Of course such an understanding is a dangerous misunderstanding.

I think it would be a serious mistake to confuse psychological therapy with spiritual direction. They are not the same. Nor is psychological health the same as holiness. However, to note distinctions is not to say that there is no connection at all between health and holiness.

Often when I think about health and holiness I think about humility. I am afraid that the teaching that I received about humility was more than a bit erroneous. We tend to think that humility involves denying any good qualities that we have instead of as seeing yourself as you really are.

Some people do not compliment others because they are afraid that they will be promoting pride. Recently I noticed that I have difficulty receiving compliments. When people say something nice about me I am delighted but I tend to interrupt the compliments or make a joke of them. It seems to me that I am afraid I will appear proud if I accept the compliment. Actually this is rather humorous. What are we supposed to do when we are complimented? Feel terrible? Unfortunately some teaching about humility has played right into people's low self-esteem. With the best intentions some preachers and teachers have encouraged us to have feelings of inferiority and to think that this is virtuous. But if humility is seeing yourself as you really are, then it has to include self-love because each of us is lovable. In fact real humility gives us a marvelous self-image. Real humility helps us to see how precious we are in God's eyes and how valuable and talented we are. To suffer from poor self-esteem is to live in falsehood rather than in truth.

Once we realize how important self-esteem is, we become more sensitive to the feelings of others. Parents have to be especially sensitive. I believe it is impossible to tell a child too often that he or she is loved or to express that love too frequently. All of us are so fragile. When God gives children to parents it is as though there is a invisible sign on the children: "Handle with care. Fragile, easily broken." That is the way that we all are. Emotional and psychic scars communicated by parents are very difficult to overcome. In fact, anyone who deals with young people should be especially sensitive to their feelings because they are in their formative years.

Even those of us who have never experienced professional counseling or therapy know what a great blessing a good listener can be. If we think about the need to have someone listen to us, we can see more deeply into a truth about personal existence: on every level of personal living I need others. I even need them emotionally. I need someone to help me be healed and to grow emotionally. I guess the person who is most emotionally troubled is the person who refuses to admit that he or she needs help. In effect such a person is preventing the healing process from happening. Such a person is denying his or her radical need. None of us is totally independent.

I am a radically needy being. In my being I am poor. All of us are. One sign of maturity is recognizing our needs and being able to take the steps that lead to their fulfillment.

Our physical needs are obvious. We need food and drink and rest and clothing. Children may not know this but we expect adults to recognize their physical needs. Someone I knew in trying to describe people who were not aware of their basic needs would say, "They don't know enough to come in out of the rain."

But in addition to physical needs we have other needs that are equally important. If we do not take care of our physical needs we will die. If we do not take care of our other needs, we may not physically die but we will not be able to have a deeply fulfilling life. Neglecting our emotional needs can lead not only to emotional problems but even psychosomatic disturbances such as ulcers, high blood pressure, asthma and even arthritis. I am not a doctor of medicine but I believe that many "physical" ailments have their source in our emotional life. The old song about the ankle bone being connected to the shin bone which is connected to the knee bone and so forth might have included the connections between our emotions and our physical health or sickness. There is a profound unity to a human being. Anything that happens to me happens not just to a part of me but always to me, the totality.

It occurs to me that the need to talk to a good listener

mirrors our dependence on God. Recognizing that we are emotionally and psychologically needy might help us to see that we are spiritually needy. In a narcissistic age this is a big step in the right direction. The good listener, the person who is able to hear us talk about our powerful emotional feelings and not reject either them or us is like God in at least two ways. The person who listens with love and does not reject us is like God in the sense that God never rejects us. God is all love. We can cut ourselves off from him but he is always offering his love to us. The good listener is like that. We should never minimize the gift that the good listener gives us. By listening with love the good listener enables us to have a new image of ourselves.

This is the second way that the good listener is like God: just by listening to us the good listener can contribute to our being healed. I find this amazing. Isn't it mind-boggling that by listening to us people can begin to heal us?

One of our greatest needs is the need for meaning in our lives. I believe that this need is not being fulfilled among large numbers in contemporary society and I think this is one of the reasons that we are experiencing a crisis in terms of the number of religious vocations. We live in a country in which the predominant philosophy is secular humanism, which claims that there is no God, that there is no supernatural, that there is no life beyond the grave, that we should do whatever good we can on earth because this is the only life we have.

Of course the problem of the lack of vocations to the religious life is complicated. I do think, however, that to the extent that the secular humanistic vision infiltrates people's understanding of life, to that extent religious life has no value or significance. Nor will religious think much of their vocations if they buy into the secular humanistic vision. I think that the crisis in religious vocations would be solved if the community believed deeply that a religious vocation was a marvelous call from God that had deep significance. The distinct value of priesthood and religious life has to be articulated as clearly as possible both for the laity and for priests and religious. As these values become more evident, one of the big obstacles to the increase of vocations to priesthood and religious life will be removed.

Because we are surrounded by the secular view of human existence, we can be brainwashed by it. We encounter it everywhere: in magazines, in newspapers, in films, on television, in popular music, in contemporary literature and theater. Because this secular vision has infiltrated so much of contemporary life it is difficult for Catholics to keep their consciousness and their consciences Catholic. It is even more difficult to grow in understanding of the faith or to deepen our insights into Christian truth. Outside of a ten-minute homily on a Sunday morning there is little to support a believer's faith.

There are at least two levels on which people need to sense that their lives have meaning: they need to sense that their life makes a difference in the world and they need to sense that their life has an ultimate meaning. Everyone wishes to feel that what he or she does is of some value. In relation to this need we should not be hesitant to praise one another because of some silly idea that we are going to lead the other person into pride. We ought to be free with our compliments. People deserve to be complimented.

For ultimate meaning we cannot believe too deeply that God loves us. That truth ought to be the radical truth of our lives. We ought to believe it passionately.

In recent years many people seem to have become more sensitive to the problems that feelings of guilt can cause. We hear people saying things like, "Don't lay a guilt trip on me!" Authors and celebrities who come from either a Catholic background or a Jewish background will talk about the strong feelings of guilt that they experienced when they were children. Some of the talk about guilt is enlightening but I think some of it is superficial and confusing. I found the treatment of guilt in Father James Sullivan's *Journey to Freedom* (Paulist Press, 1987) really fine. In simple language and with good examples Father Sullivan sheds light on both real guilt and neurotic guilt. He also offers some insights into the widespread problem of narcissism, which therapists claim is the most frequent illness that they encounter in our society at this time.

When I think about my past experience I am amazed at how confused I was about guilt feelings. When I was in grammar and high school I had enormous trouble distinguishing real guilt from neurotic guilt. Even after I was ordained I think I used people's neurotic guilt to get them to do what I thought was good for them. I wasn't aware that I was playing on people's neurotic guilt but now with hindsight I think I was.

The decline in the number of people who celebrate the sacrament of reconciliation is due to many things, some good and some not so good. One of the good things is that many people are not acting out of neurotic guilt and preachers are not playing on people's neurotic guilt. I think that one sign of maturity is the ability to distinguish between neurotic guilt and real guilt.

Concerning guilt, Father Sullivan writes: "Guilt is that extremely distressful feeling of self-blame in which I look down on myself and despise myself. It is anger at myself for some real or imagined offense that I have committed. It is looking down on myself as unworthy, ugly, bad. Often it is experienced as an absolute disgust for myself! Of its very nature, therefore, guilt diminishes my self-esteem.

"We speak of guilt as self-blame and yet in a very true sense guilt is blame from my parents, my parents whose values and ideals I have internalized to the point that they are now a part of myself. My parents' ideals and values are now part of my perceptive system in the form of locked-in filters." (p. 109)

The journey to freedom means the journey from doing or avoiding something because my parents "told" me, to doing or avoiding something because I wish to act this way. To achieve an adult conscience is no easy thing. To operate out of neurotic guilt feelings — feeling guilty when I have done nothing wrong — is to remain a dependent child.

Neurotic feelings of guilt can lead to depression and to the desire to punish self. Of course the desire to inflict pain on self, Sullivan makes clear, is really a desire to pay back for the imagined wrong and so feel good about self again. Sullivan says the ways that a person usually engages in self punishment are two: by refusing to accept love and by arranging to be hurt or injured. Of course either way is disastrous for personal growth.

We become moral adults when we take charge of our moral life. When we do something that is morally wrong, when we offend either God or neighbor or both, then guilt is a proper feeling. We blame ourselves and we ought to blame ourselves because we have done something worthy of blame.

To feel real guilt is a sign of health. Narcissists are persons who very rarely feel guilt because they have made themselves the center of the universe. Other people's feelings or rights mean little to them. I have heard therapists say that narcissists are difficult people to treat because they are so self-centered. The person who confronts or challenges them becomes the enemy — even if that person is trying to help them.

Whenever I hear counselors or psychologists speak of narcissists I hear a note of discouragement in their voices. I suspect this is because it is so difficult to break into the world of narcissists and so difficult to get them to develop a healthy relationship.

Mental health and sanctity are not the same reality. But we would be very wrong to underestimate the importance of mental health and emotional maturity for those who wish to take following Christ seriously.

A statement that Mother Teresa made several years ago made a strong impression on me. The depth of her remark is just now beginning to be clear to me. The remark was in answer to questions from people who were impressed by Mother Teresa's commitment to the poor in Calcutta. Mother Teresa said that those who wanted to do something for the poor should not come to Calcutta but should help the poor in the United States. She pointed out that the greatest poverty was spiritual poverty and that this must be dealt with if people are going to be helped. I recall that as an evidence of need, Mother Teresa mentioned the loneliness that so many contemporary people experience. Mother Teresa was correct. Her insight may be even more important today.

I suppose that I should make clear what I mean by loneliness. I do not think that loneliness has anything to do with whether your are alone or with people. People can experience loneliness when they are with other people, even when they are with large groups of people, whereas a person who is alone may not experience any loneliness at all. What is important to recognize about the experience of loneliness is that loneliness is a feeling. I think that loneliness is the feeling that I do not matter, that I do not count, that I am not significant, that no one cares about me. This feeling can be experienced by anyone — by the elderly and by the young, by the healthy and by the sick, by the single and by the married. It is difficult for me to imagine how any person can escape the feeling of loneliness completely though it is probably true that some are more subject to it than others.

Some present-day uses of the telephone highlight people's loneliness. There is a relatively new phenomenon which might be called the "group phone conversation." In 52 cities in this country it is now possible to have a phone conversation with as many as ten strangers. Numbers are advertised in a paper or magazine and people can call and either speak to strangers or engage in a conversation with them. One young man claims that the new phone service has given a new meaning to the term "blind date." Apparently the faceless encounter seems to fascinate many. According to the news story, hundreds of thousands of Americans are taking advantage of this new service. There are also "Dial-a-Porn" phone services. It is now possible to dial a phone number and either engage in an obscene conversation with someone or listen to someone present sexual fantasies to you. This type of phone service is hugely profitable. How legal it is and what restrictions the law eventually will place on it is not clear at this time. What interests me about both phone services is what they can tell us about our experience of interpersonal relationships.

Even if we allow that some of these phone calls are made out of curiosity, we still can be relatively certain that many people are having serious problems with personal relationships. Unfortunately there must be large numbers of people in our country who do not have close friends or who are not able to relate to others in any deep way. The problem is so vast that I would not be so presumptuous as to offer a solution in a brief book. But I do think that this phenomenon should cause us to pause and to reflect on how we treat people. Do we relate to people in a manner that will give them a sense of their dignity and their value as persons or do we relate to them in a way that will foster their negative feelings about themselves? Are we sensitive to the feelings of others? How do we relate to people who serve us such as sales people or subway workers or ticket collectors or waiters and waitresses? How do we relate to our fellow workers? I was in a store not long ago and I was stunned by the inhuman way that the owner dealt with one of his workers. He never spoke to her except with a loud condescending voice that seemed to carry with it the implicit question "Do you understand, stupid?"

None of us can solve the problems that hundreds of thousands of people may have with their interpersonal relationships but each of us can make a contribution that may help some of them. That kind of contribution is important. Reflecting on the two phone services, I am struck with the struggle that we have with intimacy. We want to be close to people, but we do not seem to be too successful at getting close and staying close. This is a problem shared by the married and the single, the elderly and the young. The one real sign of growth that I have observed in recent years is that people talk about intimacy more. I see this as progress because I think that people are talking about intimacy because they see the importance of it and perhaps the lack of it in their lives.

When I am referring to intimacy I am not restricting myself to sexual intimacy, though I think that this is a special problem today. There is something paradoxical about this. With all the openness in conversation about sexual matters and with all the explicit sex scenes in films and on television, we might think that no one would have a problem with sexual intimacy today. Apparently this is not the case.

Therapists and counselors report that today people have enormous problems with sexual intimacy. In spite of the so-called sexual revolution, intimacy seems no more easy to achieve than it ever was. I wrote "in spite of the sexual revolution," but perhaps I should have written "because of the sexual revolution."

I wonder if the view of sex that pervades the media today is not part of the problem with intimacy. I suspect that a person's perception of the human body and the mystery of the person incarnate in that flesh will have some effect on the person's success or failure with sexual intimacy. But the problem with intimacy goes way beyond sexual intimacy. How close can people be? What does it mean to share on a deep level? How many people do not have any close friends? Why do we have such difficulty allowing people to know what we are really like? Why do we have such difficulty revealing ourselves? If we cannot share our deepest fears and hopes with some people or at least with one person can we ever be fully human?

I suggest that a religious view of self and others could facilitate intimacy by providing a context in which people sense their value and might be more willing to reveal their deepest selves. A religious view encourages us to treat the other with respect and care and if we do this an atmosphere might be created that would encourage people to reveal their deepest selves. The attraction of others can be a call from God.

On the last line of his classic *The Diary of a Country Priest*, Georges Bernanos writes: "Grace is everywhere." One Friday night I had an almost tangible experience of that truth. During the day on this particular Friday I was teaching the doctrine of Christian existentialist Søren Kierkegaard to a class, half of which was made up of seminarians. I have taught Kierkegaard's Christian vision to so many seminarians over the last 25 years that I would not be able to guess how many. There are several reasons why I like teaching Kierkegaard to students and especially to students for the priesthood.

The Danish existentialist deals with questions of faith, commitment, freedom, relationship with God. These are questions that ought to concern all of us. My hope is that by exploring Kierkegaard's insights seminarians will begin to reflect more deeply about their own lives. Even if they do not agree completely with the father of Existentialism, and I don't, exposure to his thoughts can be a marvelous opportunity to reflect more profoundly about the most important human experiences. A teacher's dream and prayer is that something that happens in class will bear fruit later in life. Perhaps something said in class will prove to be a seed, however tiny, which will bear fruit some day in the future life of a priest. I know that when the class ended I had very positive feelings about the session.

That Friday evening I visited a prison on Long Island. How that visit came about fascinates me. A lawyer friend of mine visits the prison regularly as one of his many Christian apostolates. He claims that he started doing this because of a homily of mine that he heard. In the homily I tried to make the point that though no Christian can do everything to relieve the suffering in the world, every Christian can do something and indeed has an obligation to do something. My friend claims that the homily really spoke to him and that after Mass he began to reflect seriously about what more he could do as a follower of Jesus Christ. He decided to visit a prison and the experience has been so marvelous for him that it has become a regular part of his life.

Driving to the prison with my friend I did not know what to expect and I think I was a little nervous. He wanted me to give a talk to the prisoners, and because I had never met any of them previously I really was not sure what I should say. When we arrived in the dormitory in which about 80 prisoners lived, my friend introduced me as a priest who knew a great deal about movies, especially old movies, and he told the men, most of whom were about the same age as the seminarians whom I taught that morning, that they could ask me any question they wished about old films. I wondered whether this was a good idea. My image of prisoners was that they would not find spending a Friday evening asking some priest questions about old films a great way to spend an evening. I was surprised how much the young men followed the lawyer's lead and started throwing questions at me. This went on for at least half an hour. Finally one young man raised his hand and said, "I am really having a good time tonight. I hope that Father comes back." Everybody applauded.

When I delivered my talk I spoke about the presence of the risen Christ in the lives of each of us, and I tried to encourage the prisoners to be instruments of good when they were released from prison. Each person was in the jail for some crime connected with drugs. They lived in the same dormitory because they were part of a special program that was designed to rehabilitate them and help them to cope with the temptation to take drugs when they returned to the outside world. As I spoke everyone seemed interested in what I was saying. The impression that I had was that they were very grateful that I came to see them and to spend some time with them. This may seem strange but they reminded me of the seminarians I was with that morning. They seemed like very good people who needed some help.

Driving home I said to my friend, "They are very likable guys." My friend gently corrected me by saying, "They are lovable."

Looking back on that Friday, I marvel at the mystery of grace: I may have helped the seminarians who in the future will help others; my friend claims that I helped him; he helped me; we may have helped the prisoners; and they definitely helped us. Grace really is everywhere. Which is another way of saying God is everywhere.

~ 3 ~

Prayer:
Opening to God's Presence

Readers of this book may have had what some describe as an "ah-ha" moment of finally understanding something that you have heard much of your life. I suppose we can call such an experience an "insight." It is a strange experience because prior to the insight you may think that you have understanding, that you already grasp the ideas that are being communicated. After you have the insight your understanding seems new or at least more profound. What I am thinking of in my own life are some insights into prayer.

As far back as I can remember in my Catholic education — on the grammar and high school levels, in college and in the seminary — I was told that prayer was one of the most important human experiences. During my seminary training I spent approximately three hours a day — on some days more — in chapel in prayer. As I recall, the seminarians were encouraged to continue this prayer routine as closely as possible after they were ordained.

Of course most parish priests found duplicating the kind of

prayer schedule they had in the seminary physically impossible. Though this may be due to my misunderstanding, I believed that in relation to prayer more was always better, that quantity was as important as quality.

Carried to its extreme my view of prayer would have meant that you should spend more and more time in chapel — indeed the major portion of each day if possible. This view might make some sense if it was applied to the life of a monk or contemplative nun but it does not make sense for the rest of us. Now what seems primary to me about prayer is that we make ourselves lovingly present to God who is always lovingly present to us. Quality seems much more important than quantity.

So much of what I have heard or read in the past about the value of prayer now means a great deal to me. Reflecting on my own prayer life I think the only time I engage in prayers of petition is when people ask me to pray for some person or intention or during the prayers of petition at Mass. My personal prayer life seems to be mostly a conscious being with God. In the past my prayer life was colored — I would even say stained — by guilt feelings and a fear of God. Prayer was something that had to be done, an obligation that must be fulfilled. What should have been easy and enjoyable seemed like a burden. Thinking of prayer this way hindered any growth in my prayer life.

Those who take their Christian lives seriously ought to reflect on their prayer life at least occasionally. Praying is too important to be done slavishly or routinely. Posing questions to ourselves may be a good way of understanding our prayer life better and of improving our prayer life. Why do I pray? When do I pray? In what position is my body when I pray? Is there a reason I assume that position? What prayers do I say? Why those prayers? Do I pray formally or informally? Why do I choose either formal or informal prayer? Do I enjoy prayer? During prayer or after prayer do I experience any particular feeling? Why do I experience that feeling? Do I think that the feeling has any special significance?

Because I believe that prayer is one of our most personal experiences I hesitate to tell anyone how to pray. It strikes me a little like telling a married couple how to make love. Even if I were married I would not do that. What is most unique about a person enters the marriage relationship. I think what is most unique about us should be present when we pray. Because prayer is such an important activity it deserves our attention. If we believe it is an important activity we would be foolish not to reflect on it, examine it, evaluate it.

Everything we believe about ourselves is incarnated in the act of prayer. We at least implicitly recognize and affirm our self-identity when we pray; we explicitly recognize and affirm God as our creator and Father. If we pray to Jesus we explicitly recognize him as our savior and redeemer. Prayer can provide the proper perspective on life. It reminds us that in spite of the difficulties in our lives, even the tragedies in our lives, we depend on a God who loves us more than we can imagine.

Prayer is indispensable if we take our relationship with God seriously.

In my own life I have found centering prayer a wonderful blessing. I started doing centering prayer daily about ten years ago. The prayer has made a dramatic impact on my life. Whenever I speak publicly about prayer I mention centering prayer because I think that it is not only a wonderful way to pray but that it is especially suited for our age.

The name contains the key idea of "centering prayer." God is at the center of our being and when we pray the centering prayer we focus our attention on God present at the center of our being. We assume a comfortable position, usually sitting, choose a word that has meaning for us, for example "love" or "Jesus" or "Father" and rhythmically begin to say that word silently. We try to focus our attention on the presence of God within us. After the word has served its purpose, we may stop reciting it and just be with God. If we become distracted we should not become discouraged but rather we might start reciting the word again and re-focus on God. After the time that we have set for ourselves, for example 15 or 20 minutes, we conclude by reciting a devout *Our Father.* During the actual praying of the centering prayer we want to enjoy being with the Lord. If we recite the centering prayer every day it is quite possible that we will gradually become more aware of God's presence to us at many times during the day.

There are at least three reasons why I think that centering prayer can be especially valuable today. The first is that so many of us live at such a hectic pace that it is good to slow down in order to pray better. Centering prayer slows us down at least for some brief time during the day. The second reason is that the prayer enables us to be alone with the Lord. Centering prayer is usually prayed alone. In the centering prayer there is just God and I and I should not be afraid to be with him. The third reason is that the only purpose in centering is to be with the Lord and enjoy his company. Centering prayer is not to ask God for anything but just to be with him. I think that gives it a special value today.

At this point in my life I am a member of four discussion groups. The readings always have something to do with religion. Either the reading is theology, or popular philosophy, or literature or drama. Whatever the group tries to probe, the members are always interested in going as deeply as they can into the meaning of the reading.

What I find especially interesting is that members of the groups seem to look forward to the meeting as a very special occasion each month. I don't have to twist any arms, (or at least not more than one or two) to encourage people to attend. The meeting seems to provide a time of grace in people's hectic and somewhat secularized lives. Catholics seem to welcome the opportunity to probe more deeply into their faith and to relate their faith to their lived experience. The impression I have is that for many in the group this is the only time during their rather fast-paced lives that they have a chance to do this.

I have observed two processes happening to individuals in

the groups, especially those in a group that has been meeting for about seven years: consciousness-raising and conscience formation.

The consciousness-raising seems to be inevitable. When people gather together to discuss some serious topic can consciousness-raising be avoided? As we discuss the meaning of Jesus, the mystery of God, the meaning of faith, the mystery of love, the meaning of death, the mystery of grace and other religious topics, our consciousness is called to a new horizon. Ideas are brought up and insights are offered that an individual alone might not have. No unanimity of opinion existed when the group was started and there is none now. Nor is that a goal. The one reality that everyone shares is that all participants are Catholics. I think that all would say that their grasp of the faith has increased greatly because of their membership in the group.

In addition to consciousness-raising, the other even more interesting and encouraging phenomenon to observe, is conscience formation. Though members of the group may not agree on every topic that we discuss, everyone's conscience, including mine is challenged. For example, all of the members of the group are middle class and among them are doctors, businessmen, a nurse, lawyers, a therapist, teachers and social workers. A problem that keeps recurring is, "What can we do to help the poor? Is our lifestyle Christian or do we have and enjoy too many material benefits?" This type of question keeps emerging. As might be expected the group — as a group — has not reached an answer that is satisfactory for every member of the group. How could that happen when every person is from a different background, has his or her unique vocation, and has a lifestyle that is at least in some details different from every other person in the group? But what has happened is that some people in the group have come to a temporary decision concerning their lifestyle and they have reached that decision at least partly because of their membership in the group. They have included in their lives concrete ways to help the poor.

When I try to evaluate the various discussion groups in which I am a member I think of Jesus' words, "Whenever two or three are gathered in my name there am I in the midst of them." Thinking back on some of the sessions, I believe that some of us, perhaps many of us experienced his presence. Even if Jesus hadn't said those words we would expect him to be there. When people gather because they love him and want to know him better how could he not be there? Whenever we take a step toward Jesus it is because he has first taken a step toward us. Even though I occasionally wonder about being involved with so many groups, what happens in the groups is so inspiring that I am always amply rewarded. I receive more than I give, and I hope every member of the groups feels the same. The groups are one way of opening ourselves to God's presence.

I find the notion of God's providence mysterious. Whenever I think about God's providential presence in our lives I realize how little I understand about it. What makes God's loving providential presence especially difficult to grasp completely is our freedom. As I stated in Chapter 1, it is a big mistake to think of God's providence as turning us into automatons. We are free; we are not machines. Our freedom and God's freedom interact. How they interact we do not completely grasp. But it is a mistake to view the interaction as removing our freedom. God's presence in our lives not only does not remove our freedom but increases our freedom.

I think that it is also a mistake to think that everything that happens is the direct result of God's will. Everything in the world is not the direct result of God's will. For example, we know that sin is not the result of God's will. God does not want us to sin. I do not think that tragedies are the direct result of God's will. I do not think that God directly wills car accidents or plane crashes or diseases. Many of the things that happen in the world are the result of human freedom and that explains some of the tragedies that occur. Another source of human tragedy is that we are material and finite. Because we are material and finite we are subject to sickness and disease and physical problems and accidents. Because he has crafted a world in which there are free material human beings God allows tragedies to happen but that does not mean that he directly wills them.

There are several Christian truths that I find helpful in thinking about God's providence. The first is that God freely creates us out of love. God did not have to create us but he did create us because he loves us. God is more concerned about us than we are. God has a plan for us. He calls us to everlasting life in heaven. I do not think that every moment of our lives is planned but I do think that God is present to us every moment of our lives. Our God is never a distant God, never a disinterested observer watching us from a heavenly throne. God is involved with us every second of our lives. He is present to us constantly, loving us and calling us to deeper freedom and to a deeper relationship with him.

The Christian truth that most illuminates God's providence for me was articulated by St. Paul in Romans 8: We know that by turning everything to their good God *co-operates* with all those who love him, with all those that he has called according to his purpose. Paul's claim is amazing. God does not just work some things unto our good, God does not just turn some things to our advantage. No! God turns everything to good for those who love him. Everything! Even the most awful human experiences can lead to good because of God's love for us. The second after something goes wrong God can begin to use that event for our good. If we love God we can be sure that it will be turned toward our good. Why can we be sure? Because of God's enormous love for us. God's loving presence in our lives enables us to draw good even out of unfortunate events. Because of God's unconditional love for us there need be no ultimate human tragedy.

Most of us can probably look back on our lives and see that some events that seemed disastrous when they occurred did eventually lead to some good. Often I hear people say that though they did not see any good in some event when it occurred they eventually came to see that there was some good in it. Of course there are other events in our lives that we cannot see as good when they occur or as leading to any good ever. If we are open to God's love, he does draw good from them whether or not we can recognize or identify the good.

I suppose the best response to God's providential love in our lives is a kind of awe. God created us out of love, is present to us throughout our lives and is directing us to an eternal happiness of love. What more can we ask?

When I was a young priest in a parish I made great efforts to encourage Catholics who I knew were not attending Sunday Mass to become regular churchgoers. Back in the early sixties I was rather successful at this. My general attitude was that if I had 15 minutes alone with some Catholic I could persuade him or her of the value of Sunday Mass and probably get the person to attend Mass on Sunday. There were several reasons why I expended so much effort seeking out Catholics who did not attend Mass. One was my belief that the Mass gave graces *ex opere operato*, that is that grace came to people just by being present even if their motivations or other dispositions were not very good. I notice that now I am not as zealous in getting non-practicing Catholics to go to Sunday Mass and I am wondering why that is.

One reason is that my understanding of *ex opere operato* has changed. I still believe that the Mass gives worshippers grace. The Mass has tremendous objective value and an honestly devout participation at Mass can change a person's life dramatically. But in the past my understanding of the *ex opere operato* effects of the Mass may have been that the Mass works almost magically. I think that in the back of my mind was the notion that just by getting a person to be present physically at a Mass some marvelous transformation would take place in that individual.

My experience gradually revealed to me that this did not happen. After I would persuade — and in some instances perhaps almost bully a person to attend Mass — I often found that within a relatively short time the person stopped attending. Nothing of any depth seemed to happen in the person's life. The occasional experience of attending a Mass because of my urging did not seem to affect the person profoundly. Over a period of time I came to see that what was required in the case of many people was some kind of conversion and that without that conversion the experience of Mass would not be significantly meaningful to them — certainly not meaningful enough that they would be motivated to attend regularly.

Something else that has become more clear to me is that the presence of Christ cannot be confined to the walls of a church. The grace of Christ is available to people throughout the day. Catholics who do not attend Mass are not necessarily living without Christ. It may very well be that they are meeting him daily in other ways. I am now thinking of some Catholics I know who are not regular churchgoers and I would have to say that they seem to be very good people. Their upbringing was different from mine, their education in the faith was different from mine and their consciences are different from mine, especially concerning the sacraments. There is a real danger that I begin to think of myself as better than they are because my understanding of and attendance at Mass is better than theirs. It is quite possible that they are much closer to Jesus than I. Even though their sacramental observance of Catholicism is poor they may be following their consciences in many other ways and performing many good works. They may even have a prayer life apart from the Mass. I have to be careful not to judge those who attend Mass regularly as better persons than those who do not attend Mass regularly.

I am not trying to minimize the importance of Mass for Catholics but only calling attention to the truth that God is present to people in many ways and that how open we are to his presence depends on our conscience and our freedom. In order to help Catholics live deep sacramental lives, more is needed than "getting" them to Mass in the way that I once tried to do. To help Catholics live deep sacramental lives puts demands on many people involved in the Christian apostolate. This is why so much that is happening in parishes today is encouraging. So many people are involved in trying to build up the Body of Christ, from priests and sisters to catechists and members of parish liturgical commissions. God saves people through his Son. The rest of us try to do what we can to help ourselves and others to be receptive to God's saving graces wherever and whenever they enter our lives.

In the local Church there is a very serious problem that I

never wish to minimize: large numbers of Catholics have lost their sense of the importance of Sunday Mass. Is it due to a massive loss of faith among large numbers of Catholics? Is it due to poor catechesis? Is it one more example of how difficult it is to keep faith alive in a society that is thoroughly secular? I know that those of us who do attend Mass regularly must allow it to transform us so that we might influence others.

One of the great values in studying philosophy in college is that you are called to reflect deeply on the meaning of your life. In teaching college students at St. John's University, I try to emphasize that this is one of the benefits of studying philosophy. That philosophy calls students to the deepest type of reflection is one of the reasons that it is important that seminarians study philosophy. But it is not only college students and seminarians who should reflect on their lives. Those of us who believe that we are involved in a mysterious love affair with God should also reflect on our lives. God's Word surrounds us and through refection on this we can become better listeners and be more ready to respond to God's presence in our lives.

When I speak of God's Word I mean the risen Christ who is God's message to us. This Word is being spoken to us by God today and not just in places that we think of as holy. Unfortunately we can tend to think of God's Word as confined to the pages of Scripture or present only inside the walls of a church. Of course God's Word is in Scripture and is in a church. But the Word of God is not limited to those places. God's Word is being spoken to us in many other situations. I think that we should reflect on our daily experience and see if we can discover times and places when it is possible that God might be speaking to us.

Yesterday, before leaving to celebrate Sunday Eucharist I prayed. I think that during my prayer God's Word was present to me. I think that during my prayer it is quite possible that God was speaking to me. I know that God spoke to me during the Eucharist. While I was delivering my homily I suspect that God was speaking to me. Later in the day I went to a wake and I think that God's Word was present to me during the wake. I ended the day by going out to dinner with two friends and I suspect that I heard God's Word from my two friends during dinner. Of course, I cannot be certain about any of these messages from God but I tend to think that I am probably correct in thinking that God spoke to me. I don't think our problem is that God is not speaking to us but rather that we do not listen to him. We may be too preoccupied with our own problems and too busy telling God what we want. We have to learn to let God have our attention so that he not only listens to us but we listen to him. By reflecting on our daily experience we may be able to spot experiences when it is likely that God's Word will come to us. If we do, then we might be ready to listen and hear what God is telling us. Moments of prayer, moments with loved ones and moments with the poor are three times when it is likely that God will be speaking to us.

Perhaps one reason that we do not hear God's Word more often is due to fear. We are afraid to listen because we are afraid that God is going to ask us to do something unpleasant or to make some sacrifice. Perhaps we half-consciously think that it is better not to listen so that we will not have to do whatever it is that we think God may ask us to do. Examining my conscience I detect a real fear of listening to God. I think that the God who was presented to me in grammar school was not the God of love who is revealed in Jesus but some God whom it was impossible to please. No matter how you related to him you were going to experience discomfort because it really was impossible to please him.

Connected with this in my young mind was the constant proximity of sin. In grammar school I seem to have been surrounded by occasions of sin. I recall being afraid of committing sins that I did not even want to commit. Fear of sin and fear of God were somehow related to one another. Whoever taught me about God and sin probably had the same attitude that I had. Such an attitude dies hard.

I know that it has taken me years to change my erroneous view of God that was based on fear. I have long believed that while it is true that we are made in the image and likeness of God, we unfortunately make God in our image and likeness. What I am suggesting is that instead of allowing our view of God to be formed by Christ and his message given to us in Scripture and through his Church, we substitute our own views. There are many reasons that we do this and none of them helps us to reach the real God. For years I allowed myself to think of God as a severe judge rather than as a loving Father.

When we think of God sending his Word among us we should remind ourselves that whatever God wants to tell us he wants to tell us because of his love for us. Whatever God's message is to me it is a message of love. No matter what sacrifice God wants me to make, no matter what task God wants me to take on, he wants me to do this because he loves me. In all our dealings with him we cannot be hurt. God loves us more than we love ourselves. If I could keep this in the forefront of my mind then I would not fear listening to God's Word to me. To the extent that I believe that God is calling me in order to bless me and aid me in some way, I will not fear either hearing God's message or responding to it. Rather I will welcome God's message because I will know that God's Word is always a Word of love.

Reflecting on the presence of God's Word of love in our lives ought to move us to joy. I think that this is the ultimate attitude that we ought to have concerning God's Word: an attitude filled with joy that God wishes to be so intimately involved with us. If we study the history of religions we can see that people have always tried to put a face on God. I suppose that this is normal. Some of the faces seem very primitive to us today. Even in recent times some great thinkers have given God strange faces. How fortunate we are that God has decided to speak to us so that we are not left on our own to wonder what he is like. God in his Word, Jesus the Christ, has told us what he is like. He is our loving Father. Whenever he speaks to us he speaks as loving Father.

We do not have to go searching for God; he is searching for us. Our God is not distant. Our task is not so much to find him as to allow him to find us. While we wish to speak to him, we also should be ready to listen. We need not be afraid to listen even when the message calls for change in our lives. No matter what the message, we are listening to love.

We do not understand Jesus' resurrection completely nor do we understand our resurrection completely. We know that Jesus' resurrection freed him to be present to all people everywhere. No longer is Jesus limited by time and space. He is inviting us to open ourselves to his Father's love. We know that our resurrection will involve our fulfillment as persons.

Images of heaven are always inadequate. When children ask me what heaven will be like I try to relate images of heaven to what they love on earth. I hope it is a good idea to suggest to children that heaven will be like having Christmas every day of the year. The image of heaven that this gives them is a joyous one and one that they can understand to some extent because it is related to their experience. As adults we also want to relate our notion of risen life to what we know as fulfilling on earth. Whatever risen life is I think it must be some kind of an intensification of love. Our capacity to love and to be loved must be transformed so we experience ourselves and God and others in a new way.

When I think of the resurrection I also think of the transformation of matter. Of course our bodies will be transformed through the resurrection but I wonder if in some way all matter will be transformed. We get some hint of this happening through the sacraments. In the sacraments we get a glimpse of the importance of matter in God's plan of salvation. Through water and oil and bread and wine we are led closer to God. The sacraments can give us some sense of the importance of matter and can remind us that we are members of a religion that is based on the enfleshment of God. That the Incarnation is at the heart of Christian faith can be a reminder that there is nothing intrinsically evil about matter.

For Christians this world, in spite of all the sin in it, is not to be condemned but to be redeemed. When I think of the resurrection I think of the redemption of all matter. The resurrection suggests to me that all our efforts to make the world better are not in vain. There is no aspect of human experience and no part of the world of matter that cannot in some way experience the redemption. The motto of Pope Pius X: "Restore all things in Christ" captures beautifully the notion that I am trying to communicate. This is what Christians try to do. The effect of Jesus' death and resurrection should extend to all human activities. The distinction between the secular and the sacred should never be interpreted to mean that there are areas of material reality to which the redemption does not extend. Everything has been made new through Jesus. Grace is everywhere. The risen Christ is everywhere.

Whenever we celebrate the Eucharist, we wish to identify completely with the risen Christ and his Father. We wish to open ourselves to the action of the Holy Spirit within the

Church and indeed within each and every one of us. At times life can seem terribly difficult and all of us at one time or another become discouraged. Easter is the great sign that no matter how difficult our lives seem, God never abandons us. We are never completely alone. No matter how we feel, God is always with us. Jesus' resurrection tells us that God's love for us will see us through even death.

I think that one of the great tasks before us is making our lives integral. Often we hear people saying that they are trying to "get it all together" or that they have not been able to "get their act together." What they are referring to is what I am calling the integral dimension of our experience. Today we are pulled in many directions. Many of us live at an incredibly fast pace. We are under many and varied pressures. In the midst of these pressures we try to make as much sense of our lives as we can. At Sunday Eucharist what we hear should provide a vision of life that makes sense and that appeals to what is best in us. However, what we experience from Monday to Saturday may seem to have little or no relation to what we have heard on Sunday. Putting together into a unified whole what we hear on Sunday with what we live from Monday to Saturday is what I mean by making our lives integral.

I can recall having conversations with classmates when I was student in the seminary about the unity in a priest's life. It seemed to me that one of the most appealing aspects of a priest's life was the built-in integrity: what a priest preached and taught was built into the work that he did when he was not preaching or teaching. Whatever work a priest was involved in seemed obviously connected with the building of the Kingdom of God. After many years in the priestly ministry I still believe that the relationship between what a priest believes and the work that he does is easily seen. Unfortunately this is not true for many other people. Many people have a difficult time seeing any connection between what they believe as followers of Jesus Christ and what they spend their working hours doing. Relating what takes place at a Sunday Eucharist to what they do during the week is quite difficult for many Catholics.

One reason that Catholics have such difficulty relating what they celebrate on Sunday to what they do during the rest of the week may be due to a too rigid separation of what we understand by the sacred and the secular. It is quite possible that in stressing the importance of the Eucharist and the sacredness of everything connected with the Eucharist, we have given the impression that the holy and the sacred are confined to the Eucharist. Half-consciously we may have begun to believe that what we do on Sundays is what draws us closer to God and what we do the rest of the week is at best not leading us away from God. This rather rigid categorizing is difficult to justify in light of the Incarnation.

Catholics believe that because of the Incarnation *all* of human living has been transformed. By becoming man the Son of God made it possible for everything to lead people to his Father. There is no aspect of human living that has not been sanctified by the Incarnation. This means that work and recreation, labor and leisure, study and play and indeed all human activities can lead us closer to our heavenly Father. There is nothing so secular that it necessarily excludes the presence of the risen Lord. We have to remember this as we try to make our lives more integral.

If we forget that the risen Lord is everywhere then gradually we will allow our Monday to Saturday existence to be basically separated from what we do at Sunday Eucharist. We will allow ourselves to be swallowed up in the secular dimension of our daily existence. It will become more and more difficult for us to relate what we spend most of our time doing to what we claim we believe when we celebrate Eucharist. The sacred dimension of our daily lives will be lost.

If we isolate our Sunday celebration from the rest of the week we will shrink the meaning of what we do at the Eucharist. Very easily the practice of our faith can become narrow and self-serving. We can come to think of ourselves as the saved and those who do not celebrate the Eucharist as the great unwashed. If we isolate the Eucharistic action from the rest of our lives we will turn our faith into a private, pious practice that not only does not open us to others and the world but that makes us self-satisfied and comfortable. Relating what we do at a Sunday Eucharist to what we do the rest of the week is not easy but it is crucial in our effort to make Christ the center of our lives.

The Eucharist can serve as a model not only for the way that we pray but for the way that we live. Today one of the great tasks before Christian believers is to integrate their living and their belief. In a secular, consumer-oriented society this is no small task. Little in our society supports our faith. If we are going to integrate our life and our belief we will not get much help from the culture that surrounds us. We will have to look deeply into our religious faith and carefully analyze our experience to see how one affects the other.

Though parts of the celebration of the Eucharist are different each Sunday the basic structure of the Mass is the same. There are three parts of the structure that I think can especially help to illuminate our daily experience. In the first of the three parts we try to listen to God's word, in the second we respond and in the third God accepts and sanctifies our response.

When God's word is presented to us through Scripture and the homily we try to listen. If we are feeling well, and if the Scripture is familiar and perhaps one of our favorites, and if the homilist is interesting, then listening may be easy. However, if the Scripture is challenging and disturbing, it is quite possible that listening is not so easy. If the homilist is somehow threatening or urging us to change in a way that we do not wish to change, then listening may be extremely difficult. Whether consciously or unconsciously we have learned ways to "tune out." However when we really listen we know that we ought to respond. This is what is supposed to be happening when the gifts are offered at Mass.

The gifts of bread and wine represent us. When they are offered at Mass we are offering ourselves to our Father. Having heard his word we respond by offering ourselves. Of course the ideal is that we give ourselves as sincerely and devoutly as we can. We do not wish to hold back in any way. We really want to put ourselves at God's disposal. I think that what we are trying to do is say "Yes" to God's word as profoundly and personally as we can. I think that what we are trying to do is what Mary did when she responded to the angel's message. We are trying to say that we want our wills to be totally united to God's will. As Sunday follows Sunday we hope we are making our response better and more total.

God takes our response and sanctifies it and transforms it. The bread and wine become the Body and Blood of Christ. Our gift of ourselves is accepted by our heavenly Father and we are transformed and sanctified. We receive God's gift to us — the Body and Blood of his Son.

The basic pattern of the Sunday Mass ought to be repeated in our lives from Monday to Saturday. God's word also can come to us during the week. God's word cannot be confined to one place or one time. The word of God can come to us through our families, through our friends, through our work, through our prayer, through suffering, even through tragedy. When the word of God comes to us we want to hear it and we want to respond. That's what prayer is: hearing the word of God and responding.

If the word of God comes to us through our families or our friends we try to listen to what God is telling us. Perhaps we are not being sufficiently unselfish in relation to those we love. Or perhaps we are holding grudges. Whatever the message from God is, we want to respond. Whenever and wherever we hear God's word we try to respond. God will take our response as he takes the bread and wine at Mass and sanctify it and transform our response. We will become sanctified through God's acceptance of us and his gift of himself to us. In this way, the pattern of listening, responding and receiving God which happens in every Mass will be repeated in our Monday to Saturday lives.

Many ingredients go into the life of a person who is trying to follow Jesus Christ. Each Christian's life is unique. Though all share the same belief in God and read the same scriptures, each brings to his or her own journey many personal and even private habits and views that to some extent color his or her Christian life. What is common to everyone's Christian journey is trying to improve and deepen a loving friendship with God. Into this friendship goes just about everything in the believer's experience. I have come to believe that one extremely important factor is how a person thinks of God. The view of God that a person has can free the person magnificently or unfortunately tie the person into horrible confining knots. The face of God presented to us by Jesus is beautiful but for whatever reasons we sometimes substitute another face or miss the face that Jesus is presenting.

Recently I came across a quotation from the Catholic existentialist Gabriel Marcel that leaped off the page at me. When that happens we ought to be grateful because we have received a gift. The words of Marcel summed up a great deal of human experience for me. I think the words are not only extraordinarily comforting but also in another way quite challenging. The following is the quotation: "Hope consists in asserting that there is at the heart of being, beyond all data, beyond all inventories and all calculations, a mysterious principle which is in connivance with me, which cannot but will that which I will, if what I will deserves to be willed and is, in fact, willed by the whole of my being."

The content of this quotation is terribly important. Of course what Marcel in philosophical language is calling a "mysterious principle" the Christian identifies as God the Father. I love Marcel's expression "is in connivance with me." It's as though God is plotting with us. We are never alone, never abandoned. There is no human experience that we face completely alone. The image that comes to my mind is that God is plotting with us, almost scheming with us so that we will reach our goal. At the deepest levels of our personalities God is present, wanting what is best for us.

The words "cannot but will that which I will" might seem strange but they contain a profound truth about God. Why cannot God will that which I will when I will it with my whole being? Does this make me superior to God? Is God at my service? Of course I am not superior to God but there is a sense in which God is at my service because he has put himself at my service in the sense that he has made a commitment to me and to every person. God has tied his will to ours. He is completely for us, in favor of us. His freedom is directed in love towards our freedom. God cannot will anything that is not for our best interests. God has made a pact with us, a covenant in which he will only relate to us in love.

Whenever I instruct couples who are planning to be married, I try to make as clear as possible the idea of a covenant. The marriage relationship is unique and a Christian marriage is based on the idea of the covenant between God and his people. In a covenantal relationship what is emphasized are not rights and duties but care, concern and love. These are the ideas that ought to fill our minds when we think of God.

Not long ago I heard a preacher say that many of us have great difficulty believing that God is nothing but love. We keep suspecting that there is something more to him that is not going to be to our advantage. Think back over your own life and your own ideas of God and just see if that is not true. Many of us find it hard to believe that God is all for us, that what God wants for us is what is best for us.

At various moments of our journey toward the kingdom of God, we can be afflicted with problems that seem overwhelming. Sometimes we wonder whether we can cope. We feel as though we are going to be crushed by the burdens. The insight that is contained in the quotation from Marcel can be an enormous comfort. That God is love and is passionately in love with us is the most important truth about me and every reader of this book. Let's never forget that truth.

Conclusion

Though God's providential presence in our lives is mysterious, we can look at our lives as being surrounded by God's love. Whatever else we think about God, we believe that in relation to us God is all love. The story of our lives is a love story written by God and us, a love story involving God's freedom and our freedom. We can only move toward God because God has first moved toward us. God's love has called us into existence. God does not love us because we are; rather we are because God loves us. God's ongoing love for us invites us into community. God's reaching out, God's touching us in love makes prayer possible. Prayer which begins with God loving us, is hearing and responding to God. Prayer makes us a human community of persons who share a love relationship with the divine community of persons. Through God's loving invitation and our prayerful response, we become brothers and sisters in Christ. God is love inviting us into a personal relationship. Our loving yes is the proper response to God's loving invitation. When we say yes to that invitation, prayer has happened and we have become new persons. There is nothing more marvelous than love and prayer. The community of prayer that includes God and us is nothing but love.

Published by Resurrection Press

Discovering Your Light *Margaret O'Brien*	$6.95
The Gift of the Dove *Joan M. Jones, PCPA*	$3.95
Healing through the Mass *Robert DeGrandis, SSJ*	$7.95
His Healing Touch *Michael Buckley*	$7.95
Of Life and Love *James P. Lisante*	$5.95
A Celebration of Life *Anthony Padovano*	$7.95
Miracle in the Marketplace *Henry Libersat*	$5.95
Give Them Shelter *Michael Moran*	$6.95
Heart Business *Dolores Torrell*	$6.95
A Path to Hope *John Dillon*	$5.95
The Healing of the Religious Life *Faricy/Blackborow*	$6.95
Transformed by Love *Margaret Magdalen, CSMV*	$5.95
RVC Liturgical Series: The Liturgy of the Hours	$3.95
The Lector's Ministry	$3.95
Behold the Man *Judy Marley, SFO*	$3.50
I Shall Be Raised Up	$2.25
From the Weaver's Loom *Donald Hanson*	$7.95
In the Power of the Spirit *Kevin Ranaghan*	$6.95
Young People and...You Know What *William O'Malley*	$3.50
Lights in the Darkness *Ave Clark, O.P.*	$8.95
Practicing the Prayer of Presence *van Kaam/Muto*	$7.95
5-Minute Miracles *Linda Schubert*	$3.95
Faith Means *Antoinette Bosco*	$3.50

Spirit-Life Audiocassette Collection

Witnessing to Gospel Values *Paul Surlis*	$6.95
Celebrating the Vision of Vatican II *Michael Himes*	$6.95
Hail Virgin Mother *Robert Lauder*	$6.95
Praying on Your Feet *Robert Lauder*	$6.95
Annulment: Healing-Hope-New Life *Thomas Molloy*	$6.95
Life After Divorce *Tom Hartman*	$6.95
Path to Hope *John Dillon*	$6.95
Thank You Lord! *McGuire/DeAngelis*	$8.95

Resurrection Press books and cassettes are available in your local religious bookstore. If you want to be on our mailing list for our up-to-date announcements, please write or phone:

Resurrection Press
P.O. Box 248, Williston Park, NY 11596
1-800-89 BOOKS